From

Penguin Books Australia Ltd
487 Maroondah Highway, PO Box 257
Ringwood, Victoria 3134, Australia
Penguin Books Ltd
Harmondsworth, Middlesex, England
Viking Penguin, A Division of Penguin Books USA Inc.
375 Hudson Street, New York, New York 10014, USA
Penguin Books Canada Limited
10 Alcorn Avenue, Toronto, Ontario, Canada M4V 3B2
Penguin Books (NZ) Ltd
Cnr Rosedale and Airborne Roads, Albany, Auckland, New Zealand

First published by Penguin Books Australia Ltd 2000

1 3 5 7 9 10 8 6 4 2

This collection copyright © Penguin Books Australia Ltd 2000

Cover image: *Silent Night*, Viggo Johansen (1851–1935)
Reproduced with permission of the State Library of Victoria
Cover design by Sandy Cull, Penguin Design Studio
Text design by Ellie Exarchos, Penguin Design Studio
Typeset in 10.5/16 pt Centaur by Post Pre-press Group, Brisbane, Queensland
Printed in Australia by Australian Print Group

National Library of Australia
Cataloguing-in-Publication data:

The little book of Christmas.

ISBN 0 14 029941 6.

Christmas.

394.2663

www.penguin.com.au

The Little Book of
CHRISTMAS

PENGUIN BOOKS

At Christmas play and make good cheer
For Christmas comes but once a year.

THOMAS TRUSSER

CHRISTMAS IS:

Flaming puddings
The smell of pine trees
Fairy lights
Christmas window displays

'Twas the night before Christmas,
when all through the house
Not a creature was stirring — not even a mouse:
The stockings were hung by the chimney with care,
In hopes that St Nicholas soon would be there.

CLEMENT C. MOORE

Joseph, son of David, do not fear to take
Mary as your wife, for that which is
conceived in her is of the Holy Spirit; she
will bear a son, and you shall call him Jesus,
for he will save his people from their sins.

MATTHEW 1: 20—21

WHO IS SANTA?

St Nicholas was the original Father Christmas. In the 4th century, he was the bishop of Myra (now part of Turkey) and saved the town from starvation. Over the centuries he has become the red-suited, ho-ho-ho-ing man we love as Santa Claus (an abbreviation of St Nicholas).

The birth of Christ was first celebrated
on 25 December in 4th-century Rome.

The word 'Christmas' comes from
the Old English *Crīstes mæsse*,
meaning mass of Christ.

Midnight mass on Christmas Eve is
perhaps the most important celebration
on the Christian calendar. In the
5th century the Pope led the first
service at Santa Maria Maggiore,
one of Rome's most beautiful churches.

The child born on Christmas Day will have a special fortune.

OLD PROVERB

Before Christianity 25 December was
widely celebrated as the pagan festival of
the winter solstice, which honoured the
return of the Sun God. There was much
rejoicing as the days grew longer,
signalling the coming of spring.

In Italy *La Befana* is the kindly witch who flies around on her broomstick at Christmas time to deliver presents to all the children.

... and she gave birth to her first-born son
and wrapped him in swaddling clothes and
laid him in a manger, because there was no
place for them in the inn.

LUKE 2:7

The Three Wise Men were in fact astrologers sent by King Herod, ruler of Galilee, to find the child who was said to be born the King of the Jews.

Oh little town of Bethlehem
How still we see thee lie.
Above thy deep and dreamless sleep
The silent stars go by.

CHRISTMAS CAROL

Wassail, n. I. a festivity or revel with drinking of healths. 2. alcoholic drink for toasting on festive occasions, *esp.* spiced ale, as on Christmas Eve and Twelfth Night.

CHRISTMAS PUNCH

4 cups orange juice
6 cups cranberry juice
2 cups lemonade
½ cup brown sugar
3 teaspoons whole cloves
3 teaspoons ground allspice
1 whole nutmeg, crushed
cinnamon sticks

Tie the spices in a piece of cheesecloth. Place the bundle in a saucepan and add the other ingredients. Bring to a boil, stirring often. Cover and reduce heat. Simmer for 30 minutes. Serve warm in dainty mugs or in long-stemmed glasses.

The Christmas Rose

According to legend a poor shepherd
girl, having no gift for the infant Jesus,
was visited by an angel who caused the
Christmas rose to spring from the frozen
soil of Bethlehem and burst into bloom.
This was then her gift for the new baby.

Buon Natale

Italian for 'Merry Christmas'

Hark the Herald Angels sing
Glory to the new-born King
Peace on Earth and mercy mild
God and sinners reconciled ...

CHRISTMAS CAROL

Looking for a gift with a difference this Christmas? Give the gifts of the Three Wise Men: something in gold, frankincense (available as essential oil) and myrrh.

THE CHRISTMAS STAR

A shooting star? A meteor? A comet?
A miracle?

Astronomers today still wonder about the star that was believed to have appeared at the time of Jesus' birth. The exact time of His birth is not known, but astronomers cannot place a new star's appearance anywhere near the possible time.

*A clear star-filled sky on Christmas Eve
will bring good crops in the summer.*

OLD GREEK PROVERB

Germany first celebrated Christmas
in 813 in the city of Mainz.

Deck the halls with boughs of holly
Fa-la-la-la-la, la-la-la-la
'Tis the season to be jolly
Fa-la-la-la-la, la-la-la-la

CHRISTMAS CAROL

During the Roman Empire the custom of decorating buildings with evergreens at New Year was widespread. The present-day custom of hanging wreaths and garlands on doors comes from this ancient ritual.

POMANDERS

Pierce holes all over a small, thin-skinned orange with a skewer. Insert a whole clove into each hole. Place the orange in a bag with one tablespoon of ground orrisroot and shake until the orange is covered. Store in the bag in a warm, dark place for three weeks.

Select ornate braids and ribbons to tie around the pomander. Hang them on the Christmas tree, around the house or use them as a table decoration. After Christmas, hang the pomander in a cupboard or place in a drawer for sweetly fragranced clothes.

King Hakon the Good established
Christmas in Norway around the middle
of the 10th century.

Bells and firelight and candles and children,
waits and the deep bassoon, and the bare
English fields and woodlands, hooded with
snow, night at the window, Sirius up aloft,
and the fires of the frost smouldering
under the moon.

WALTER DE LA MARE

In north Germany, to remain true to
the religious sentiments of Christmas,
it is the Christ Child himself,
Christkind, who traditionally delivers
presents to the children.

Nadolig Llawen

Welsh for 'Merry Christmas'

A Swedish Christmas

St Lucy's Day (13 December) marks the
beginning of the Christmas festivities in
Sweden. Traditionally, at the first
cockcrow, the prettiest girl in the house
dresses in a white robe and wears a wire
crown with nine candles fastened on it.
She then wakens all the people in the
house with fresh sweet coffee.

Spread Christmas cheer to those less fortunate by contributing to community food and toy collections.

Away in a manger, no crib for a bed
The little Lord Jesus lay down His sweet head.
The stars in the bright sky look down where
He lay —
The little Lord Jesus asleep on the hay.

CHRISTMAS CAROL
(lyrics by Martin Luther)

In 1224 St Francis of Assisi recreated
the nativity scene with a real ox and ass,
as he had seen done on his travels in the
Holy Land. From then on it became a
popular custom.

Many cultures follow the tradition of setting out a crib on the dining table, under the Christmas tree or on the mantel. Traditionally the crib is left empty until 25 December when a baby doll is placed in it to symbolise the arrival of baby Jesus.

Ding Dong merrily on high,
In heav'n the bells are ringing.
Ding Dong verily the sky
Is riv'n with angels singing.

CHRISTMAS CAROL

In some countries the celebration of the Epiphany on 6 January has even more significance than Christmas. This is the day the Three Wise Men arrived in Bethlehem to worship the baby Jesus.

In the Middle Ages Christmas was
twelve days of celebration. Epiphany
marked the closure of the festive season.

In 1521 the first Christmas tree as we know it, decorated with coloured balls and miniature figures, appeared in Alsace, then a part of Germany.

With its prickly leaves, holly has always been associated with the crown of thorns. A German legend claims that before the crucifixion the holly plant bore white berries, but afterwards its berries were blood red.

*You might as well do your Christmas
hinting early.*

ANON.

In the late 16th century, Martin Luther is said to have decorated a small Christmas tree with candles to show his children how the stars twinkled at night.

MULLED WINE

1 orange, sliced and seeded

½ cup sugar

2 cups water

1 teaspoon ground cloves

2 teaspoons cinnamon

1 bottle red wine

Combine the orange, sugar, water and spices in a large stainless-steel or enamelled pot. Slowly bring to the boil, reduce heat and simmer for 15 minutes. Reduce heat again, add the wine, and slowly reheat, but do not boil. Serve warm in mugs.

Hyvää Joulua

Finnish for 'Merry Christmas'

Legend has it that long ago some spiders stealthily entered a very fussy woman's house and climbed all over the Christmas tree, but the Christ Child turned the cobwebs into decorative silver tinsel so that the woman would not be angry.

Plant Christmas lily bulbs in May so
they are blooming for Christmas.
Bulbs planted in pots make beautiful,
inexpensive gifts or interesting
table decorations.

Knecht Ruprecht is an ominous figure
who appears at Christmas time in
Germany. Draped in skins and straw, he
quizzes the children on their prayers.
If they can recite them, he rewards
them with gingerbread; if they can not,
they are punished.

Brown paper and string make very striking wrapping. Their simplicity can belie the nature of the present!

Silent Night, Holy Night
All is calm, all is bright,
Round yon virgin mother and child,
Holy infant so tender and mild,
Sleep in heavenly peace
Sleep in heavenly peace.

CHRISTMAS CAROL

Choose some really beautiful fabric
to make into Christmas stockings.
If you are worried that all your presents
won't fit into a stocking, leave out a
special pillowslip.

Love came down at Christmas,
Love all lovely, Love divine;
Love was born at Christmas,
Star and angels gave the sign.

CHRISTINA ROSSETTI

On the Twelfth Day of Christmas

My true love sent to me

Twelve lords a-leaping

Eleven ladies dancing

Ten pipers piping

Nine drummers drumming

Eight maids a-milking

Seven swans a-swimming

Six geese a-laying

Five gold rings

Four colly birds

Three French hens

Two turtledoves

And a partridge in a pear tree

CHRISTMAS SONG

Mele Kalikimaka

Hawaiian for 'Merry Christmas'

In 1645 the puritan government in England banned Christmas and declared it a working day. People who were found making Christmas pies were sometimes arrested as an example to others.

MAKE YOUR OWN ANGEL STENCIL

Trace around the shape opposite,
transfer the angel onto a piece of folded
paper or card, with the edge of the angel
aligned with the fold. Cut around the
outline. Unfold the paper and you will
have a whole angel to paste onto a card
or to spray-paint around to create
heavenly paper.

According to custom the Christmas pudding should be prepared with thirteen ingredients to represent Christ and His disciples. Every member of the family should take turns to stir the pudding with a wooden spoon from east to west, in honour of the Three Wise Men.

'Figgy Pudding' was a mixture of meat and figs. Over time, oats replaced the meat and the pudding became a sweet porridge. In the 17th century, ground almonds, fruits, nuts and flour were added to the mixture, which was then boiled within a cloth and hung and dried for several months to mature before serving.

For a truly rich, mature Christmas pudding, make your pudding at least three months in advance and water it with extra brandy from time to time.

Brandy butter makes a delicious topping
for your Christmas pudding. Cream
75 grams of butter with 175 grams of
caster sugar until pale and smooth. Little
by little add 2–3 tablespoons of brandy.
Beat well after each addition. Chill before
serving with piping-hot pudding.

Little Jack Horner sat in the corner
Eating a Christmas pie.
He put in his thumb, and pulled out a plum,
And said, 'What a good boy am I!'

NURSERY RHYME

Instead of hanging plastic wreaths, make an environmentally friendly wreath for your door from fresh or dried foliage and pine cones or gum nuts.

In 1742 Handel's *Messiah* was performed
for the first time, in Dublin. The words
of this beautiful, epic oratoria are from
the Bible.

In 1840 Princess Hélène of
Mecklenburg, Germany, brings
Parisians their first Christmas tree.

In France the main Christmas celebration, *le réveillon*, occurs on Christmas Eve. Families gather, go to midnight mass and open all their presents on Christmas Eve.

Père Noël visits children in France and
fills their stockings with all things good.

Make Christmas presents personal: dip your baby's or child's hand or foot in paint and stamp it onto paper. Name, date and frame the artwork each year. It makes a lovely present for grandparents.

It was always a great treat for English children to find an orange in the toe of their Christmas stocking, for in years gone by this fruit was a rare, expensive item.

Joyeux Noël

French for 'Merry Christmas'

The yule log was ceremoniously felled
by families throughout Europe and
brought into the house on Christmas
Eve to burn for the twelve days of
Christmas. The ash of this log is
thought to be imbued with special
powers of healing and good fortune.

Bûche de Noël is the name of the French
Christmas cake – a chocolate sponge
rolled up with a cream filling to
resemble a log.

Good luck will come to the home where a fire is kept burning throughout the Christmas season.

OLD ENGLISH PROVERB

Heap on more wood! — the wind is chill;
But let it whistle as it will,
We'll keep our Christmas merry still.

SIR WALTER SCOTT

Celebrate the approach of Christmas
with a really special Advent calendar
with good-quality chocolates inside.
A lovely treat for big and little
children alike.

In 1841 Prince Albert (originally from Germany), husband of Queen Victoria, set up the first Christmas tree in England, at Windsor Castle. From the royal court the custom of Christmas trees spread quickly to the middle class and then to working people.

The story of Santa Claus and his reindeer arrived in England at the same time.

In Victorian times in England no Christmas Day was complete without a game of charades. Today, this is the perfect way to aid the digestive processes after an enormous lunch!

To create a festive atmosphere at home,
stock your pantry with treats in the
weeks leading to Christmas. Bowls of
nuts in their shells with a traditional
nutcracker make an appetising display.

Try different themes for the Christmas tree each year: decorate it with gingerbread shapes or cover it entirely with silver decorations. Instead of a traditional tree, spray long branches of twisted willow with gold paint and decorate with ribbons and small lanterns.

You will have as many happy months in the coming year as the number of houses you eat mince pies in during Christmas time.

OLD ENGLISH PROVERB

CHRISTMAS BALLS

1 cup dates
1 cup mixed walnuts and almonds
¼ cup preserved figs or raisins
¼ cup preserved ginger
1 cup sultanas
1 cup desiccated coconut
½ tin condensed milk
extra coconut for coating
glacé cherries for topping

Chop dates, nuts, figs and ginger. Add sultanas and coconut, then condensed milk, mixing well. Mould a teaspoon at a time into balls, roll in coconut. Press to form a peak on top with a piece of cherry. Bake on a greased tray in a moderate oven for 15–20 minutes. Cool slightly on tray before removing.

A potted, miniature Christmas tree can
thrive in the garden for eleven months of
the year and then be decorated every
Christmas season.

In parts of England and Wales it was customary for farmers to give mistletoe to the first cow that calved in the New Year. This was thought to bring good luck to the entire herd.

God rest you merry gentlemen,
Let nothing you dismay;
Remember Christ our Saviour,
Was born on Christmas Day.

CHRISTMAS CAROL

Before the modern postal system, carols were a way of sending a Christmas greeting. Carol singing, especially on Christmas Eve, is still a very popular custom in many countries, with the singers moving from house to house.

'I am the Ghost of Christmas Past.'
'Long past?' inquired Scrooge ...
'No. Your past.'

CHARLES DICKENS

A lovely American tradition is to invite
friends and family over to help you
decorate the tree on 1 December.
Everyone brings (or makes) a
decoration to hang, and so the
Christmas season begins.

Christmas is coming, the geese are getting fat,
Please put a penny in the old man's hat;
If you haven't got a penny, a ha'penny will do,
If you haven't got a ha'penny, God bless you!

BEGGAR'S RHYME

For gorgeous-looking presents, wrap them in stencilled tissue paper. Simply place a dried leaf, or a stencil of a snowflake, angel or star on the paper and spray with gold or silver paint.

GOOD PRESENTS FOR GIRLS:

A voucher for a facial

Beautiful writing paper

Subscription to a magazine

Silk flowers

GOOD PRESENTS FOR BOYS:

A voucher for a foot massage

A set of thank-you cards

A book voucher

Chocolates

It came upon the midnight clear,
That glorious song of old,
From angels bending near the earth,
To touch their harps of gold!

CHRISTMAS CAROL

Rudolph is the most famous reindeer of all. He was terribly embarrassed about his bright, shiny nose until, one day, Father Christmas came looking for someone to light the way for his sleigh through the night.

'What did Adam say on the day
before Christmas?'

'It's Christmas, Eve.'

Traditionally in Poland, instead of sending Christmas cards, special biscuits with figures stamped on them were exchanged between friends.

WHITE CHRISTMAS

2 cups rice bubbles
1 cup mixed fruit
1 cup desiccated coconut
1 cup icing sugar
1 cup powdered milk (dry powder)
vanilla essence
225 grams copha shortening

Place rice bubbles, fruit, coconut, sugar,
powdered milk and vanilla in a bowl.
Slowly melt the copha over a gentle heat
and combine with other ingredients.
Mix well. Press into a slice tin to set.
Chill before cutting into finger-length
pieces for serving.

It was not until 1862 that the sending of Christmas cards became common practice. In England, highly decorative writing paper was the precursor to Christmas cards.

Sit down to write Christmas cards
early, and take the time to write
personalised and meaningful messages
to family and friends.

CHRISTMAS IS:

Office parties
Hot mince pies
Mounds of wrapping paper
Christmas crackers with paper hats

Handmade Christmas cards are easy to make and are a delight for the receiver. Cut a large potato in half, then carve a star shape into the flat surface. Dip the potato in gold or silver paint and stamp it on a piece of brightly coloured card.

Miracle on 34th Street (1947) is probably the most famous Christmas film. Santa Claus goes on trial to prove he is the real thing to a disbelieving child. The miracles of Christmas never cease.

'Jingle Bells' is still the song played
most frequently in America during
the Christmas season.

Egg Nog

6 eggs

1 cup sugar

pinch of salt

1 cup golden rum

900 ml cream

600 ml milk

nutmeg

Beat eggs until light and foamy. Add sugar and salt and beat until thick. Stir in rum, cream and milk. Chill for at least three hours and serve with a sprinkle of nutmeg.

*I stopped believing in Santa Claus when
I was six. Mother took me to see him
in a department store and he asked me
for my autograph.*

SHIRLEY TEMPLE

Kriss Kringle is a great way of giving presents in the workplace or in large families. Everybody draws a name from a hat and then must give an inexpensive present anonymously to that person.

According to Russian legend it is
Baboushka, a kindly old woman, who
delivers presents to the children at
Christmas time.

Can you name all the reindeer?

Dasher

Dancer

Prancer

Vixen

Comet

Cupid

Donner

Blitzen and ...

Rudolph!

Jutdlime pivdluarit ukiortame
pivdluaritlo

Eskimo for 'Merry Christmas'

CHRISTMAS GAMES

Make a papier-mâché reindeer and fill it
with sweets. Hang it from a tree, then
take it in turns to try to hit the reindeer
while blindfolded. Make sure everyone
has a bag handy, so that when the
reindeer finally breaks open you have
somewhere to stash the sweets.

'Mum, can I have a parrot for Christmas?'

'No, you'll have turkey like the rest of us.'
Ho! Ho! Ho!

Boxing Day, 26 December, is named for an old tradition. Boxes were placed in churches for offerings of goodwill and the contents were distributed by priests among the needy the day after Christmas.

Geseënde Kersfees

Afrikaans for 'Merry Christmas'

In Irish homes a candle is lit and placed in the window each night during Advent to show Mary and Jesus the way to a warm home, and to welcome the baby Jesus.

'White Christmas' is still one of the best-loved Christmas tunes. Written by Irving Berlin in 1942, this song was made famous by the dulcet tones of Bing Crosby.

In most Greek homes gifts are exchanged on 1 January, St Basil's Day. Dried figs are traditional Christmas food, served with the spicy golden *Chrisopsomo* bread.

One-stop Christmas shopping is ideal
for the busy person. Try a nursery for
potted fruit trees and garden ornaments,
a bookshop for all manner of books
and diaries, or a food hall for
delectable morsels.

Father Christmas loves a mince pie
or two, a glass of milk or a small
swig of whisky. Leave some outside
your bedroom door for him on
Christmas Eve.

Don't forget to leave out food for Santa's
reindeer, either. They love fresh hay,
grated carrot or a crisp red apple.

Kissing under the mistletoe is a tradition
that is still fervently maintained.
In ancient times, the Druids believed
that mistletoe had life-giving powers,
and in Scandinavia it was also said
that this plant could bestow great
powers of fertility.

Good Christmas Music:

Handel's *Messiah*

Bach's *Christmas Oratorio*

Aled Jones, the world's most
famous choirboy

Charlotte Church, an angelic voice from
Wales, the land of song

Glad tidings we bring
To you and your kin;
We wish you a Merry Christmas
And a Happy New Year!

CHRISTMAS SONG

In the Christmas ballet *The Nutcracker*,
Clara is given a wooden nutcracker in
the form of a soldier on Christmas Eve.
That night she dreams that the soldier is
real and they fall in love. She wakes up
to find her dream has come true.

In Greece it is a tradition to burn old shoes during the Christmas season to prevent misfortunes in the coming year.

Again at Christmas did we weave
The holly round the Christmas hearth;
The silent snow possess'd the earth,
And calmly fell our Christmas Eve.

ALFRED, LORD TENNYSON

CHRISTMAS POTPOURRI

3 cups dried red rose petals

10 small pine cones

1 tablespoon whole cloves

4 cinnamon sticks

1 cup star anise

1 tablespoon ground nutmeg

1 tablespoon ground cloves

1 tablespoon ground cinnamon

2 tablespoons allspice berries

Gently mix all the ingredients until well combined. Seal in an airtight jar and leave for eight weeks, shaking jar gently daily. Arrange in a shallow bowl as a centrepiece, or put in a decorative box to make a thoughtful present.

Good King Wenceslas looked out
on the feast of Stephen;
When the snow lay round about,
deep and crisp and even.
Brightly shone the moon that night,
though the frost was cruel,
When a poor man came in sight,
gathering winter fuel.

CHRISTMAS CAROL

Priatnogo Rozhdestva

Russian for 'Merry Christmas'

In Ethiopia Christmas is celebrated on
7 January, in ancient churches carved
from solid volcanic rock.

Stir a dash of brandy through fresh double cream to dollop onto Christmas pudding. An easy alternative to brandy sauce, and just as delicious.

In Norway Santa Claus has so many
presents to deliver on Christmas Eve
that he must employ a little helper,
Kriss Kringle.

Leave out a token of goodwill for the postie or newspaper deliverer. Giving some bottles of beer to your local garbage collectors is also a gesture of good cheer.

Bonu nadale

Sardinian for 'Merry Christmas'

For a dramatic table centrepiece, cover the tips of pine cones with Epsom salts to create the effect of snow. Use clear glue under the salts. Arrange the pine cones on a mirror for twice the effect.

Home life, as we all remember at Christmas, is life at its best. There, in the trust and love of parents and children, brothers and sisters, we learn of how men and nations too may live together in unity and peace.

So to every one of you who are gathered now
in your homes or holding the thought of home
in your hearts, I say — a merry Christmas
and God bless you all.

KING GEORGE VI, FROM HIS MAJESTY'S
BROADCAST ON CHRISTMAS DAY 1946

In the Victorian era a good Christmas tree would be six branches tall. It was decorated with garlands, candies and paper flowers, and placed on a table covered with a white damask tablecloth.

Write a cheerful letter to Santa well
in advance of Christmas Eve and leave
it in a visible place around the house so
that he can be sure to know what gifts
to leave you.

ALMOND ROCCA

Individually wrapped in cellophane
parcels, this makes a great gift.

1 cup blanched almonds, chopped
¾ cup brown (not raw) sugar
½ cup butter
½ cup semisweet chocolate chips

Spread almonds on bottom of greased slice tray. Heat sugar and butter until boiling, stir constantly for 7 minutes. Remove from heat and spread mixture evenly over almonds. Melt the chocolate pieces and spread over the toffee. Cut into squares while still hot. Place in fridge until firm.

Raymond Briggs' Father Christmas, in his story of the same name, is one of our best-loved characters, despite being a grumpy old man who doesn't want to get out of bed to deliver the presents!

Feliz Navidad y Próspero Año Nuevo

Colombian for 'Merry Christmas
and a Happy New Year'

Make Christmas an adventure for
small children by hiding presents
around the house for them to find
on Christmas morning.

It is an old tradition to add small
objects to the Christmas pudding
mixture. These indicated whether good
or bad luck would greet the finder in
the year ahead. To find a ring meant
marriage, a thimble or a button that
you would stay single, while a small
coin promised wealth.

If you feel that you can't face one more
year of turkey and plum pudding,
organise a seafood extravaganza, a
Moroccan banquet, or, in warm climes,
an *al fresco* picnic.